Data Collection and Analysis in Hostile Environments

Dr. Horen Kuecuekyan

Technics Publications

SEDONA, ARIZONA

115 Linda Vista, Sedona, AZ 86336 USA
https://www.TechnicsPub.com

Edited by Jamie Hoberman
Cover design by Lorena Molinari

First Printing 2025

Copyright © 2025 by Dr. Horen Kuecuekyan

ISBN, print ed.	9781634626231
ISBN, Kindle ed.	9781634626286
ISBN, PDF ed.	9781634626293

Library of Congress Control Number: 2024952290

Contents

CHAPTER ONE

Foundation

O ver the past several decades, the practice of data collection has undergone a transformative evolution. Initially, it was limited to simple manual recording methods, but it has since progressed to sophisticated digital systems capable of gathering vast amounts of information in real-time. While revolutionary in its impact on research and decision-making, this evolution has been accompanied by increasingly complex challenges, particularly when operating in hostile environments.

In the early days of systematic data collection, researchers and practitioners predominantly employed manual methods, including paper forms, in-person interviews, and direct observations. While labor-intensive and resource-demanding, these traditional approaches established the groundwork for comprehending the fundamental principles of data gathering accuracy, consistency, and relevance. The mid-20th century witnessed the gradual introduction of mechanical and early electronic devices, representing the initial substantial shift toward automated data collection.

The advent of personal computers in the 1980s revolutionized the field, introducing novel possibilities for data storage and analysis. However, it was not until the 1990s and early 2000s that networked systems commenced to transform our approach to data collection in challenging environments. This period heralded the advent of real-time data gathering and remote monitoring capabilities, although these systems were often costly and necessitated substantial technical expertise for operation.

The advent of the digital revolution has fundamentally transformed the data collection landscape. The proliferation of mobile devices, sensors, and Internet of Things (IoT) technology has created unprecedented opportunities for gathering information from even the most challenging environments. Today's data collection tools encompass sophisticated satellite systems and miniature sensors capable of being deployed in harsh conditions, often operating autonomously for extended periods.

This technological evolution has also democratized data collection, enabling smaller organizations and individual researchers to gather high-quality data at scale. However, this democratization has presented its own challenges, particularly in terms of data quality control and validation. The ease of data collection has sometimes resulted in an overwhelming volume of information, not all of which meets the necessary standards for scientific or operational use.

The concept of hostile environments has undergone a substantial expansion in the digital era. Historically, hostile environments were predominantly physical, encompassing war zones, disaster areas, and regions with extreme weather conditions. While these challenges persist, we now also face novel forms of hostility that can be equally detrimental to data collection endeavors.

Physical hostile environments continue to pose significant challenges for data collection. These environments include active conflict zones where infrastructure is damaged or unreliable.

Natural disaster areas where normal access routes are compromised and regions with extreme weather conditions that can damage equipment, plus remote locations with limited accessibility and resource availability, create challenges we must solve.

> *In such environments, the physical safety of both personnel and equipment becomes paramount, often necessitating innovative approaches to data collection that minimize human exposure while ensuring data integrity.*

The advent of digital hostile environments presents a novel challenge in data collection. These environments encompass sophisticated cyber threats and active adversaries.

The areas with substantial electromagnetic interference and regions with substantial digital surveillance and monitoring need location-specific solutions as well as locations where digital communications are restricted or monitored.

Digital hostility manifests in diverse forms, including deliberate signal jamming and sophisticated cyber-attacks intended to corrupt or steal collected data. These threats necessitate the development of novel protocols and technologies for secure data collection and transmission.

The most intricate form of hostile environment is social hostility, which arises from human factors and poses substantial challenges to data collection.

We must treat regions with stringent regulatory or political restrictions on data gathering and areas where cultural norms restrict access to specific populations or information differently.

There will also be locations with robust resistance to external observation or monitoring and environments where trust concerns significantly hinder data collection endeavors.

Addressing social hostility necessitates not only technical solutions, but also sophisticated approaches to fostering trust and ensuring cultural sensitivity while upholding scientific rigor.

The convergence of various forms of hostility has necessitated the development of novel methodologies and approaches to data collection.

Contemporary data collection systems must be resilient to multiple forms of interference and attack and adaptable to rapidly evolving conditions. A very important consideration is to be able to operate with minimal human intervention while at the same time being able to validate and verify data in real time. The design needs to consider inherent redundancy and fail-safe operations.

Organizations engaged in data collection in hostile environments must consider a comprehensive matrix of threats and challenges, frequently necessitating hybrid approaches that amalgamate conventional methods with cutting-edge technology. This has catalyzed the development of sophisticated risk assessment frameworks and adaptive collection strategies that can dynamically respond to changing conditions in real time.

Furthermore, the imperative for reliable data acquisition from hostile environments has catalyzed innovation in several pivotal domains:

- Developing robust sensors and data collection devices using novel protocols for secure data transmission.

- Implementing sophisticated encryption and authentication algorithms is required, as well as the design of autonomous and semi-autonomous collection systems integrated into AI-driven validation and verification tools.

The field continues to evolve at an accelerated pace, with novel challenges emerging as technological advancements and the evolving nature of hostile environments unfold.

Comprehending this dynamic landscape is paramount for individuals engaged in data collection, as it serves as the bedrock for developing effective strategies and selecting suitable tools and methodologies.

Contemporary Challenges in Hostile Environment Data Collection

Gathering data in hostile environments presents a distinct set of challenges that transcend conventional data-gathering complexities. These challenges necessitate meticulous consideration and innovative solutions to guarantee both the quality of the collected data and the safety of those involved in its acquisition.

Security and Safety Considerations

The paramount concern in hostile environment data collection is the security and safety of personnel, equipment, and data. Physical security threats can range from direct violence in conflict zones to environmental hazards in disaster areas. Personnel operating in these environments must often balance the need for comprehensive data collection against immediate safety concerns.

Implementing security protocols has become increasingly sophisticated, incorporating real-time threat assessment systems with dynamic risk mapping and avoidance strategies.

> *Emergency evacuation procedures need to be integrated into data collection protocols with secure communication channels for field personnel and redundant safety systems and fail-safes.*

Equipment security presents another critical challenge. Modern data collection devices must be hardened against both physical and electronic threats. This includes protection against extreme environmental conditions (temperature, humidity, pressure). Physical tampering and theft, electronic interference and jamming, cyber-attacks, and data interception with power fluctuations and outages are minimal operational environments to create.

> *Maintaining data integrity in hostile environments presents unique challenges that require innovative solutions.*

Data Collection Accuracy

Data collected under duress or in challenging conditions may be susceptible to various forms of degradation or corruption. Organizations must implement robust validation mechanisms to ensure data integrity, including real-time data quality checks. We must use multiple redundant collection methods, each integrated into cross-validation capabilities with alternative data sources. We must also establish automated error detection and correction systems along with regular calibration and verification procedures.

Chain of Custody

Maintaining a transparent chain of custody for collected data is paramount, especially when utilizing data for critical decision-making or legal proceedings. This necessitates comprehensive documentation of collection procedures, including secure timestamping and location tracking.

Digital signatures and encryption are basic requirements, as well as blockchain or similar immutable record-keeping systems with regular audits and verification processes.

Ethical Considerations and Compliance in Hostile Environments

The ethical considerations surrounding data collection in hostile environments are intricate and multifaceted.

Securing genuine informed consent in such environments presents distinct challenges, particularly when collaborating with vulnerable populations is part of the task. Operating in regions with limited literacy or education needs to be properly addressed, such as engaging with communities experiencing stress or duress.

In environments characterized by language and cultural barriers, meticulous consideration is important to ensure a successful operation. Individuals tasked with data collection should be equipped to navigate potentially tense situations while maintaining the integrity of the collection process. Individuals employed in such settings must possess not only proficiency in the local language but also a comprehensive understanding of regional dialects, non-verbal communication cues, local customs, social hierarchies, religious practices, and cultural sensitivities. These team members should be trusted and be able to mitigate the risk of unintentional offense. Furthermore, they should receive training in conflict-aware communication techniques, enabling them to discern appropriate levels of directness and indirectness in their interactions. The recruitment and training of personnel with this multifaceted cultural and linguistic expertise serve as a cornerstone in ensuring the accuracy of data collection while minimizing risks to both the research team and the local participants.

Robust privacy protection measures are required in hostile environments where data exposure poses significant risks. These measures encompass implementing stringent anonymization protocols and ensuring secure data storage and transmission.

Establishing transparent protocols for data access and sharing, conducting regular privacy impact assessments, and adhering to compliance with diverse jurisdictional regulations are required.

Traditional and Modern Methods

The evolution of data collection in hostile environments has led to a sophisticated fusion of traditional and modern approaches, creating hybrid methodologies that leverage strengths while mitigating their respective weaknesses.

Traditional data collection methods hold considerable value, especially when technology infrastructure is unreliable or non-existent.

Local customs and practices may favor personal interaction and digital solutions could draw unwanted attention. Trust-building and verification are paramount to data collection success. Augment these traditional approaches through digital documentation of manual collections and mobile tools for field notes and observations.

Hybrid interview techniques that combine personal interaction with digital recording can significantly enhance data quality.

Integration of local knowledge with scientific data collection in combination with the development of culturally sensitive collection protocols can help to consolidate the data set.

Modern technology, particularly the Internet of Things (IoT) and Sensor Networks, have revolutionized data collection.

IoT devices and sensor networks enable continuous monitoring of environmental conditions in hostile environments, providing real-time tracking of critical parameters and automated alerts for abnormal conditions.

Integrating multiple data streams with comprehensive analysis reduces the need for human presence in dangerous areas.

Advanced remote sensing capabilities have expanded the scope of data collection through satellite imagery and analysis, drone-based data gathering, and LiDAR and radar systems. Also, multispectral and hyperspectral imaging and acoustic and seismic monitoring would add very important information to the set.

The progress of mobile and distributed data collection systems has catalyzed the emergence of novel opportunities, such as resilient data transmission networks for uninterrupted data flow (Mesh Networks). Furthermore, edge computing has enabled localized data processing to be more efficient by fully utilizing available resources, including mobile devices, which facilitate data collection in the field.

Highly distributed data storage systems with redundancy where required, opened the capability for real-time synchronization across locations.

The integration of emerging technologies continues to reshape the field through Artificial Intelligence (AI) and Machine Learning (ML). These tools can clean and validate the data in almost real-time. They can apply pattern recognition techniques and anomaly detection for predictive analytics, including risk assessment.

Natural Language Processing (NLP) opens the data collection across language barriers, which is required for more reliable decision support systems.

Blockchain and Distributed Ledger Technologies can enhance immutable data recording. Smart contracts and a transparent chain of custody ensure automated compliance and distributed data verification.

The data for analysis and results can have a variety of sensitivity levels, from sensitive to top secret or TS-SCI.[1]

Sharing the information needs to be automatically segmented. Information added at a sensitive level can, during the processing of additional data, reach the highest levels of security. The backpropagation of the information needs complex segmenting processing for sharing and storage. Any individual has to be able to see data and results aligned with her/his clearance level to receive the required information without compromising the full sensitivity level.

> *The successful integration of these various methods requires careful consideration of available local context and conditions as well as available infrastructure and resources.*

The data quality and security requirements have to be consistent with the sustainability and maintenance of the system deployed at every level.

This convergence of methods has created a more robust and adaptable approach to data collection in hostile environments.

---

[1] Top Secret Sensitive Compartmented Information (TS/SCI) is a security clearance level and information access designation used within the United States intelligence community and other government agencies. It represents one of the highest levels of security clearances in the U.S. government system.

However, it also necessitates greater expertise and more sophisticated management systems to implement effectively.

Analysis View

The transition from data collection to meaningful analysis presents unique challenges in hostile environments, particularly when leveraging machine learning techniques. Understanding these challenges and establishing proper foundations is crucial for successfully implementing ML-based analysis systems.

In hostile environments, organizations frequently encounter a fundamental tension between data quality and quantity, significantly impacting the implementation of machine learning (ML) algorithms. This paradox manifests in several key ways:

- The quality of data collected in hostile environments is frequently compromised.

- There are operational restrictions like inconsistent measurement conditions. The equipment degradation under harsh conditions is a real concern. Sensors can be affected by the environment or inference from external sources. There are very rare access points to calibration facilities.

- Time is always a huge factor during collection, which almost eliminates the ability to verify the input in the field. Access to collection sites may be limited or restricted by collection protocols.

- There is a significant compromise by incomplete or interrupted data collection.

Human Factors and Quantity Requirements

Collection by humans can induce errors caused by stress in the operational area, with communication barriers hindering the recording. The validation depends on the expertise and training of the collector. Cultural factors may impact accuracy as well as safety.

Data Volume and Distribution Considerations

Specific requirements will determine the sampling methodology to encompass a wide range of conditions. A comprehensive dataset will possess the requisite variations for a reliable analysis.

Edge cases and anomalies should be collected as well as extended with seasonal and temporal variations. Uneven distribution of the data across various conditions impacts the analysis and needs adjustment during the process.

Temporal discontinuities in the data, over and under-representation of critical but challenging-to-collect data, and gaps in the collection, must be considered and compensated through algorithmic adjustment.

Successfully implementing ML in hostile environment data analysis requires careful attention to several key prerequisites:

- We must establish a robust data infrastructure by standardizing collection protocols and multi-level quality control mechanisms. Error detection has to happen automatically.

- Secure data warehousing protocols must be followed by the storage on highly distributed systems.

- Audit trails are very important for the processing. As we need to identify obfuscated objects without data loss, complex version control mechanisms must be part of the inference to follow backward references. We should consider edge computing and cloud integration where feasible.

- As a highly sensitive environment, we need to establish high-performance role-based controls. Encryption at rest and in transit with secure authentication systems and data integrity is a basic requirement.

Data Preparation

Machine Learning implementation success hinges critically on robust data preparation and systematic processing approaches. At its foundation, the process begins with comprehensive data cleaning and validation protocols. This includes sophisticated anomaly detection systems that automatically flag irregular patterns alongside systematic approaches for handling missing data points. Organizations must establish consistency checking mechanisms and standardize data formats across their systems to ensure reliable analysis.

Feature engineering represents another crucial component of the ML pipeline. This process involves carefully extracting domain-specific features while employing automated selection methods to identify the most relevant data points. Advanced dimension reduction techniques help manage complexity, while proper scaling and normalization ensure data consistency. For time-series applications, we must give special attention to creating meaningful temporal features that capture important trends and patterns.

Bridging Data Collection and Analysis

The connection between data collection and analysis requires a sophisticated architecture that handles both real-time and batch-processing needs. Real-time processing systems must incorporate stream processing capabilities with online learning integration, allowing for immediate validation checks and ' dynamic adjustments as conditions change. These systems need robust error handling and recovery protocols to maintain continuous operation.

Batch processing systems complement real-time operations by enabling efficient data aggregation and integration of historical data. These systems support periodic model retraining procedures and comprehensive quality assurance protocols, ensuring that the ML system maintains its effectiveness over time.

Integration and Workflow Management

Successful system integration depends on maintaining strict compatibility standards across all components. This includes standardized APIs, consistent data formats, and aligned protocols across different tools and platforms. We must carefully manage version compatibility to prevent system conflicts.

Workflow management becomes increasingly critical as systems scale. Modern ML implementations require sophisticated process automation with built-in error handling and quality control checkpoints. Comprehensive documentation and audit trails ensure transparency and facilitate system maintenance.

Industry Standards and Best Practices

Current industry best practices emphasize strong data governance frameworks. Quality management systems must incorporate specific metrics for data quality, along with continuous monitoring and improvement protocols. Compliance and ethics considerations have become increasingly important, with specific attention paid to regulatory requirements, privacy protection, and security standards.

We must clearly document and consistently follow operational standards. This includes detailed protocols for data collection and processing, along with comprehensive analysis methodologies. Organizations need to maintain robust training programs and support systems to ensure personnel can effectively operate and maintain the ML infrastructure.

Performance Monitoring and Optimization

Effective ML systems require continuous monitoring of both technical and operational performance metrics. Technical monitoring includes tracking algorithm accuracy, processing efficiency, and system reliability. Operational monitoring focuses on collection success rates, processing throughput, and overall cost-effectiveness.

The dynamic nature of ML implementation in challenging environments requires organizations to maintain flexibility while ensuring system integrity. Regular reviews and updates of approaches, technologies, and procedures help maintain system effectiveness and resilience in the face of evolving challenges and opportunities.

This comprehensive approach to ML implementation creates a robust framework that can adapt to unique challenges while maintaining high standards of data quality and analytical integrity. As the field continues to evolve, organizations must stay current with emerging technologies and best practices to ensure their systems remain effective and competitive.

The successful implementation of ML-based analysis in hostile environments requires careful attention to all these elements, creating a comprehensive framework that can handle the unique challenges while maintaining data quality and analytical integrity. Organizations must regularly review and update their approaches as new technologies emerge and circumstances change, ensuring their systems remain effective and resilient.

CHAPTER TWO

Concepts

Following the objective of this book, diverse aspects of data collection will be evaluated, thereby creating a balanced and transparent dataset that reveals any discernible biases. As Chapter 1 explained, there are significant challenges besides data collection.

Step-by-step through the chapters, we will develop a comprehensive outline of data collection principles for analysis purposes. Subsequently, we will apply machine learning algorithms to identify abnormal patterns in event planning or incident management.

Data mining and inference using machine learning algorithms are the same in hostile and non-hostile environments. The only difference is that hostile environments add an extra dimension to the process. In both cases, we deal with a lot of available information. In non-hostile environments, the information is mainly clear and easy to understand, or at least concise.

A hostile approach conceals and obfuscates data, rendering it challenging to identify, isolate, and analyze objects. Conversely, benign data facilitates more efficient mining. Hostile data entails multiple modified versions of the same information to evade traceability, substantially hindering the mining process due to the multiplicity of virtual objects.

Hostile activities entail additional preprocessing layers and mining steps to consolidate a data set for algorithmic analysis.

These preprocessing steps are of paramount importance. Normal data may inadvertently introduce obfuscation, necessitating analysis and review to establish a reliable data set for mining.

For instance, we analyze data over a short or broad time window, identifying objects and their properties. Inter-object relationships are substantial patterns for the inference engine. In a hostile environment, we may isolate and track ten objects over time and analyze their relationships to each other and to the remaining data space. In a later phase, we may discover additional information to reduce the former ten objects down to two individual entities.

In contrast, we must reverse the analysis and the cross-dependencies from ten individual entities to two. The complexity is evident, as the inference is not linear and may have generated a network of interactions.

The details and approach to address these issues will follow in subsequent chapters. The rationale behind selecting data collection in hostile environments at the outset remains unchanged. Once we address these issues, the subsequent inference steps for normal or hostile data will remain consistent.

In the mining analysis process, we will explore various machine learning tools, including GANs (Generative Adversary Networks) and any capabilities offered by LLMs (Large Language Models).

Data Collection Details in Conflict Zones

Collecting data in conflict zones and politically unstable regions is a critical yet complex task for humanitarian organizations, researchers, journalists, and governments.

> *The data gathered from these areas is invaluable for decision-making, resource allocation, policy formulation, and insights into the human impact of conflicts.*

However, the volatile nature of these regions presents unique challenges, including safety risks, accessibility issues, ethical concerns, and data reliability problems. This chapter delves into the methodologies, challenges, and considerations involved in data collection in conflict zones, emphasizing the importance of such data and offering insights into best practices to enhance the quality and safety of data collection efforts.

This book's two appendices provide a more detailed description of two conflict and war zones. These appendices include a brief historical overview. While they are not essential to comprehend the book's content, they offer additional information. The intricate interplay of various factors, which may not be immediately apparent, significantly influences the environment and presents challenges in data collection and analysis within these regions.

The first area examines the trajectory and evolution of the Afghanistan War, delving into the intricate ethnic dynamics and development with the election of the first president that have transpired over the years.

The second area focuses on the international standing of Iraq, examining its development prior to the Iraq invasion. It also provides a five-year snapshot encompassing the war and its subsequent post-war phase.

These areas were selected because they provide a diverse range of available data sources between HUMINT (Human Intelligence) and SIGINT (Signal Intelligence).

Human Intelligence, or HUMINT, involves gathering information through direct human interaction, including espionage, interviews, interrogations, and even observations in conflict zones. While the fundamental principles of HUMINT have remained relatively consistent, the approach has undergone significant evolution due to advancements in technology, geopolitical shifts, and alterations in the tactics employed by contemporary intelligence targets.

HUMINT, in the first case, primarily relied on traditional espionage and in-person human interactions, along with physical document handling. Field operatives and case officers used common practices to establish and maintain networks of assets (informants) in target regions. These officers were trained in clandestine operations, tradecraft, and counter-surveillance techniques.

Establishing trust with assets necessitated a substantial investment of time and resources. Operatives frequently spent years undercover in a region to acquire valuable information. Information was often exchanged through face-to-face meetings or physical methods such as dead drops (concealed locations for leaving messages or items). Communications with assets were meticulously managed to evade detection, and meetings necessitated sophisticated counter-surveillance to prevent exposing the asset or officer.

A substantial emphasis was placed on gathering intelligence from hostile nations and governments.

Intelligence gathering primarily targeted traditional state actors, military secrets, and political developments, particularly in regions such as the Middle East and Eastern Europe, which were perceived as high-risk geopolitical zones. The primary targets of this intelligence-gathering effort were government officials, diplomats, military personnel, and defectors.

Technology support was limited, necessitating a heavy reliance on face-to-face communication. Digital communication and remote handling were less secure due to these constraints. Surveillance equipment, such as micro-cameras and recording devices, was utilized sparingly due to its limited availability and heightened risk of detection.

In conflict zones, interrogations and direct questioning were the primary methods of gathering intelligence. Prisoners of war, defectors, or suspected agents were commonly interrogated to extract critical information.

The two pictures on the next page show the outpost of the US as far east as possible in West Berlin's Teufelsberg in the fifties.

The surveillance station was tasked with the most sophisticated equipment available at the time to listen to communication, analyze in various languages, and communicate constantly the findings to US military as well as to data collection agencies including the NSA. More than 100 people were onsite during regular operations.

In the context of technological advancements and a shifting global landscape, modern human intelligence (HUMINT) has evolved to embrace novel tools and adapt to the evolving behavior of targets. HUMINT increasingly utilizes encrypted digital communication to recruit and manage assets remotely, often bypassing the necessity for direct contact. Secure messaging applications, encrypted emails, and specialized communication software facilitate interactions with sources across borders.

Digital identities and online aliases (also referred to as "cyber personas") are frequently employed to engage with potential sources, particularly in regions where physical presence poses risks. Social media platforms provide valuable data for HUMINT operations, enabling agents to monitor targets' activities, recruit assets, and conduct background checks online.

Intelligence agencies also utilize Open-Source Intelligence (OSINT) to complement HUMINT by gathering information from publicly available sources and employing data analytics to identify trends or potential leads.

Modern operatives can effectively utilize tools, such as facial recognition, GPS tracking, and biometric identification to monitor individuals discreetly. These technologies facilitate the verification of identities and enhance surveillance of potential threats without the need for direct observation.

Current HUMINT operations encompass a diverse range of targets, including non-state actors such as terrorist organizations, organized crime groups, and influential individuals. The decentralized nature of contemporary threats has necessitated a broader scope of HUMINT targets.

Field operatives increasingly engage with Non-Governmental Organizations (NGOs), religious leaders, and influential business figures, particularly in regions of strategic political or economic importance. Recruiting and managing sources through online methods has become increasingly prevalent, especially in countries where agents face restrictions on their physical presence. Online identities enable operatives to establish connections under the pretense of a different nationality or organization, facilitating rapport-building in hostile environments.

Artificial intelligence (AI) and machine learning (ML) have now been integrated into HUMINT operations. By analyzing behavioral data, predictive algorithms can assist in identifying potential informants or assessing the reliability of assets based on communication patterns and previous interactions.

AI-driven tools analyze social media profiles and digital footprints to derive insights into personality traits, political ideologies, and social networks.

HUMINT increasingly collaborates with other intelligence disciplines. For instance, signals intelligence (SIGINT) is often employed to validate information obtained from human sources, while open-source intelligence (OSINT) provides contextual information to enhance fieldwork effectiveness. Some operatives now receive specialized training in cyber and technical skills to facilitate initial contact through digital methods, even if a mission ultimately necessitates in-person engagement.

All these changes, including the evolution of methods, sources, and resources, do not eliminate significant challenges. Digital counter-surveillance has become quite prevalent. The widespread use of surveillance technology and digital forensics facilitates the identification and blocking of communications by targets, thereby increasing the risks to operatives and assets. Determining the trustworthiness of digital sources has become more challenging, as it is easier for individuals to present false identities online.

Thanks to enhanced training and technology, numerous state and non-state actors have become increasingly adept at detecting and eliminating foreign intelligence activities.

> *Human intelligence has become a fusion of traditional tradecraft and advanced digital techniques, aiming to adapt to a rapidly evolving online environment. This evolution reflects both the complexity of contemporary global threats and the technological tools available for human intelligence gathering in the present day.*

Signal Intelligence (SIGINT) encompasses the interception and analysis of signals, encompassing both communications and electronic emissions, for intelligence-gathering purposes. Historically, SIGINT encompasses two primary domains: Communications Intelligence (COMINT), which involves intercepting verbal or written communication, and Electronic Intelligence (ELINT), which focuses on non-communication signals such as radar or weapon system frequencies. Over the past two decades, SIGINT approaches have evolved significantly due to technological advancements, data processing capabilities, and communication methods.

In the context of the recent historical environment, SIGINT primarily focused on intercepting conventional analog and digital communication methods, including radio, satellite transmissions, and wired telecommunications.

A substantial portion of early SIGINT efforts involved intercepting radio frequencies and satellite communications. These communications were often unencrypted or utilized relatively simple encryption methods. Agencies deployed large satellite dishes and radio towers globally to intercept signals. These installations were frequently situated in remote or restricted areas to minimize interference and detection.

Wiretapping of phone lines, cellular networks, and internet traffic was prevalent, often with direct cooperation from telecommunications providers. Landline phone interception was relatively straightforward, while mobile networks were predominantly utilizing 2G (GSM), which possessed limited encryption capabilities.

Due to limited computing power, data analysis was predominantly manual or based on algorithms that did not require high computing resources. Agencies prioritized high-value targets and utilized extensive manpower to sift through intercepted information. Large data centers were constructed to store intercepted communications, but the processing and searching capabilities were slower and more resource-intensive than contemporary technology.

SIGINT collection frequently necessitated physical access to the source or at least proximity to signal emitters. Consequently, a significant portion of interception relied on physical listening posts or on-ground operatives. Intercepted data was often encrypted, and while agencies possessed decryption capabilities, the process was time-consuming. This limitation restricted the availability of real-time intelligence from encrypted sources.

The altered environment presents novel opportunities amidst modified challenges.

With the rapid pace of technological advancements, SIGINT has undergone a transformation into a more sophisticated, automated, and data-driven discipline. Cyber SIGINT has adapted to the expansion of internet-based communications, shifting its focus to monitoring online platforms, encrypted messaging applications, and social media.

Agencies now employ advanced cyber infiltration techniques, such as compromising network infrastructure, to gain access to data before encryption or to insert malware for persistent access. SIGINT has expanded to encompass data from a wide range of sources and utilizes automated machine learning and artificial intelligence (AI) to analyze vast datasets rapidly.

Real-time language processing, pattern recognition, and predictive analysis enable agencies to identify threats more swiftly and with greater accuracy. Modern SIGINT has developed more sophisticated decryption methods, often employing dedicated hardware such as quantum computing prototypes or specialized algorithms for breaking encryption.

Agencies frequently circumvent encryption by intercepting data at vulnerable points, such as end devices or before encryption (for instance, through collaborative efforts with technology companies or utilizing backdoors). Remote surveillance technologies now permit interception from vast distances without necessitating proximity to signal sources.

Drones, satellites, and sophisticated airborne surveillance platforms now collect signals across expansive areas, augmenting reach while maintaining covertness. The proliferation of Internet of Things (IoT) devices, GPS, and wireless technologies has augmented SIGINT sources. Devices such as smartphones, connected cars, and even smart appliances emit signals that disclose location data, patterns of life, and communication habits. SIGINT encompasses monitoring various "non-communication" signals, which may encompass metadata from IoT, GPS, and environmental sensors.

Cloud-based storage and processing infrastructure facilitate agencies in managing and analyzing terabytes of intercepted data in near-real-time.

Real-time language translation and sentiment analysis enable agencies to discern pertinent information from global communications at scale.

Signals Intelligence (SIGINT) capabilities have become more potent yet encounter distinct challenges:

- The advent of novel encryption methods, particularly end-to-end encryption in messaging applications, poses substantial obstacles to SIGINT.

- The exponential influx of data can be overwhelming, rendering it challenging to discern truly pertinent intelligence.

- Counter-surveillance technologies, such as Virtual Private Networks (VPNs), encrypted messaging, and secure browsers complicate data collection.

In essence, the evolution of SIGINT from conventional methods to the contemporary high-tech milieu demonstrates a clear shift toward more sophisticated, automated, and distributed intelligence gathering—oriented toward addressing the challenges of contemporary communications and data security.

Data collected from conflict zones provides crucial information on the immediate needs of affected populations, including food security, healthcare, water, sanitation, and shelter requirements. This data enables humanitarian organizations to prioritize aid delivery, allocate resources efficiently, and tailor their interventions to the specific needs of different communities, for example, during the Syrian Civil War that began in March 2011. Data on internally displaced persons (IDPs) and refugees helped NGOs and international agencies coordinate their efforts, ensuring that aid reached the most vulnerable groups.

If data from the collected area is a military intervention space, all precautions can be planned by knowing the hostility density and distribution of red forces. It is important to protect humans in the military as well as civilians around the operation. The data can be used to analyze and predict the short- and medium-term change. In the best case, the extracted information can be used to start peace negotiations or at least plan the path in the short term. Data on human rights abuses and civilian casualties can be instrumental in advocating for ceasefires, sanctions, or international humanitarian interventions. Advocacy groups rely on robust data to raise awareness, mobilize resources, and press for accountability from governments and armed groups.

If this is a disaster zone, policymakers in local, national, and international sectors will use the information to assist the affected population.

Data collection is essential for understanding the dynamics, causes, and impacts of conflicts. By analyzing data on conflict-related events, such as armed clashes, civilian casualties, and displacement patterns, researchers and peace-building organizations can gain insights into the drivers of conflict and identify potential pathways to resolution. This information is vital for conflict resolution efforts, peace-building initiatives, and the prevention of future conflicts.

Data Collection Challenges

Safety Risks

One of the most significant data collections challenges in conflict zones is the security risk to data collectors and respondents. Armed violence, kidnappings, landmines, and other threats make data collection dangerous. Humanitarian workers, journalists, and researchers often face the risk of being targeted by armed groups who may perceive them as threats or adversaries. Ensuring the safety of all involved is a primary concern, and sometimes, data collection efforts are limited or halted due to escalating violence. For example, in Yemen, ongoing conflict and security risks have severely restricted access to affected areas, making it difficult to collect reliable data on the humanitarian situation.

Infrastructure and Access

Conflict often destroys infrastructure, including roads, bridges, and communication networks, complicating access to conflict zones. These disruptions make it challenging to reach affected populations and can hinder the transportation of data collection tools and personnel. Additionally, the lack of electricity, internet access, and other basic services can impede the use of digital data collection methods. In remote areas of the Democratic Republic of Congo (DRC), poor infrastructure has made it difficult for data collectors to reach communities affected by conflict, limiting the scope of data collected.

Bias and Reliability

The chaotic nature of conflict zones can result in unreliable data. Respondents may be unwilling or unable to provide accurate information due to fear, trauma, or mistrust of outsiders. Moreover, using biased sampling methods, such as only surveying individuals in easily accessible areas, can lead to skewed data that does not accurately represent the broader population. Interviewer bias, where the data collector's presence or questioning style influences responses, can also affect data quality. In Afghanistan, for example, cultural barriers and mistrust of foreign data collectors have sometimes led to incomplete or biased data on civilian casualties and humanitarian needs.

Ethical Aspects

Ethical considerations are paramount when collecting data in conflict zones. The principle of "do no harm" must guide all data collection activities, ensuring that the process does not put respondents at risk or exacerbate their vulnerabilities. We must carefully manage issues of consent, confidentiality, and the potential misuse of data. For instance, collecting personal data without proper safeguards can expose individuals to reprisals from armed groups or government forces. In Syria, concerns about data misuse have led to heightened scrutiny of data collection efforts, with some organizations adopting more stringent ethical protocols to protect respondents.

Methodologies for Data Collection

Remote Collection

Remote data collection methods, such as satellite imagery, drones, and remote sensing, offer valuable alternatives when physical access to conflict zones is not feasible. These technologies can provide high-resolution images of conflict-affected areas, allowing for the monitoring of population movements, infrastructure damage, and environmental impacts without endangering data collectors. For instance, during the conflict in the Ukraine, satellite imagery was used to monitor the destruction of civilian infrastructure and assess the displacement of populations in real time.

Digital Tools

Mobile phones and digital platforms have revolutionized data collection in conflict zones. Tools such as SMS surveys, mobile apps, and social media monitoring enable data collectors to gather information from respondents while minimizing direct contact. Mobile-based data collection methods are particularly useful in environments where traditional face-to-face interviews are not possible due to security concerns. For example, in Somalia, mobile surveys have been used to collect data on food security and displacement, providing timely information to humanitarian agencies despite ongoing conflict.

Community Approaches

Community-based data collection involves engaging local communities in the data collection process. This approach leverages local knowledge and networks, allowing for more contextually appropriate and culturally sensitive data collection. Community-based methods can include participatory mapping, focus group discussions, and key informant interviews with local leaders and community members. In conflict-affected regions of Nigeria, community-based approaches have been used to gather data on the impact of armed group activities on local populations, helping to inform community-driven responses to the conflict.

Techniques for Hostile Environments

Risk Management and Assessment

Conducting thorough risk assessments is critical in preparing for data collection in conflict zones. Risk assessments should identify potential threats to data collectors and respondents, including physical security risks, health hazards, and legal or political risks. Developing comprehensive risk management plans that include contingency planning, security protocols, and regular monitoring of the security situation can help mitigate these risks. Organizations should also have clear evacuation and communication plans in place for data collectors operating in high-risk areas.

Capacity Building

Providing training on security, ethics, and data collection methodologies is essential for data collectors working in conflict zones. Training should cover topics such as personal security, situational awareness, first aid, and how to handle sensitive information. Building the capacity of local data collectors is also crucial, as they are often better positioned to navigate the challenges of conflict zones. Local data collectors typically have a deeper understanding of the cultural and social dynamics of their communities and are more likely to be trusted by respondents.

Consent and Ethical Frameworks

Adhering to ethical frameworks is fundamental to responsible data collection in conflict zones. This includes obtaining informed consent from respondents, protecting their anonymity and confidentiality, and ensuring that data collection does not cause harm. Ethical considerations should also address the potential misuse of data, particularly in contexts where information could be used to target vulnerable populations. Organizations should implement robust data protection measures, such as encryption and secure data storage, to safeguard sensitive information.

Innovative Technologies

Leveraging technology and innovative approaches can enhance data collection efforts in conflict zones. For example, blockchain technology can be used to secure data and ensure its integrity, while artificial intelligence (AI) can assist in analyzing large datasets and identifying patterns that might not be immediately apparent. Cloud-based platforms can facilitate data storage and sharing, allowing for real-time collaboration among organizations working in the field. In the Central African Republic, AI and machine learning have enabled the analysis of social media data to monitor conflict dynamics and inform early warning systems.

Data collection in conflict zones and politically unstable regions is fraught with challenges but remains essential for understanding and addressing the needs of affected populations. Organizations can navigate the complexities of these environments by employing a combination of remote, digital, and community-based methods and adhering to best practices in risk management, ethics, and technology use. The data collected plays a critical role in shaping humanitarian responses, informing policy decisions, and contributing to conflict resolution and peace-building efforts.

As the world continues to grapple with the impacts of conflicts, the importance of reliable and ethical data collection cannot be overstated.

CHAPTER THREE

Assessment

D ata mining systems use a variety of algorithms and generate millions of patterns. Reliable, reproducible patterns are knowledge. This requires data preprocessing steps, providing a transparent and reliable source to feed the algorithms. Preparing the data that will be used to feed various algorithms is extremely important, tedious, and very time-consuming. To obtain qualitative and reliable results, the data must be evenly distributed and properly balanced before processing. This ensures a stable foundation for algorithms to execute their steps systematically.

The fundamental principle remains valid: if we input poor-quality data, we will obtain unreliable results. Similarly, an analysis based on flawed or inaccurate data cannot yield trustworthy insights.

The Significance of Data Preprocessing

Data preprocessing is a major step in enhancing the quality or discarding specific datasets to create a base balanced with a known quantitative matrix. It creates the foundation for extracting meaningful and reproducible knowledge from raw data. This chapter delves into the importance of data preprocessing, its various techniques, and how it contributes to the overall success of data mining projects.

Data mining systems employ a wide array of algorithms to generate millions of patterns from input data. However, not all patterns are equally valuable or reliable. The goal is to identify reproducible patterns that can be considered knowledge. To achieve this, the data fed into these algorithms must be of high quality, consistent, and free from noise and inconsistencies.

Datasets often contain missing attributes or attribute values or containing aggregates of some values. These can lead to skewed results if not handled properly. Discrepancies created by using different coding systems used to categorize the content or labeling or data entry errors, can significantly impact the accuracy of data mining results. Random errors or variations in measured variables and noise can obscure the underlying patterns in the data.

Datasets with a large number of attributes can create extremely high-dimensional datasets and increase computational complexity. This may potentially lead to less meaningful results.

Data normalization facilitates the comparison of disparate variables by scaling them to a comparable range, typically between 0 and 1. This process is fundamental to accurate analysis. By employing distance measurements, such as Euclidean or Manhattan distance between data points, we can identify and address outliers, evaluate data consistency, and guarantee that all features contribute proportionally to the analysis. This standardization procedure is indispensable for maintaining data quality and ensuring reliable outcomes, especially when dealing with diverse datasets that encompass variables measured in disparate units.

An important preprocessing step is data reduction, which reduces the data size by aggregating and eliminating redundant features.

There are various approaches to enhance the quality of the dataset.

Data Cleaning

The first fundamental step in preprocessing is the cleaning of the entire dataset.

Address the missing values. If possible and only with feasible human interaction, missing global attributes can be manually added. Replace all missing values with a well-defined global constant that machine learning algorithms can distinguish and identify. A refined algorithm can iteratively handle the global constant consistently.

Measures of central tendency would indicate the middle of the data distribution, such as mean, median, and mode. The mean is the preferred approach for numerical attributes in a normal or symmetrical data distribution. For skewed data distributions, media should be used for numerical data. Categorical values should be substituted with mode.

Determine the most probable values by regression, inference-based tools grounding on Bayesian formalism, or decision tree induction. Using other attributes in the dataset to construct a decision tree would fill the missing values.

If applicable, replacing or ignoring missing values by applying review and inference tools from the dataset is the best method. Algorithmic substitution of missing values from the dataset can provide inter-data dependencies.

Outliers in the Dataset

If a value in the dataset is an extremely high or extremely low data point relative to the nearest data point and the rest of the neighboring values, this is an outlier. The basic rules for defining an outlier are:

- For a low outlier, the data point needs to fall more than 1.5 times the interquartile range below the first quartile.

- A data point that falls more than 1.5 times the interquartile range above the third quartile is considered a high outlier.

Two fundamental statistical approaches are widely employed to identify outliers in the data: the interquartile range (IQR) method and the z-score method. The IQR method divides the data into four equal intervals and calculates the spread between the first quartile (25th percentile) and the third quartile (75th percentile). Any data points that exceed 1.5 times the IQR above the third quartile or fall below the first quartile are designated as outliers.

In contrast, the z-score method assesses the distance of a data point from the mean. Typically, values with a z-score exceeding 3 or below -3 (indicating three standard deviations from the mean) are considered potential outliers.

Outlier detection by clustering methods assumes that the normal data objects belong to large and dense clusters, outliers belong to small and sparse clusters, or do not belong to any clusters.

When grouping similar data points together, three prominent clustering algorithms emerge, each possessing distinct advantages. **K-means** clustering divides data into a predetermined number of clusters ('k'), where each data point is assigned to the cluster with the closest center. It iteratively adjusts these centers until the optimal grouping is achieved, making it suitable for datasets with a known number of clusters and spherical cluster shapes.

DBSCAN (Density-Based Spatial Clustering of Applications with Noise) employs a distinct methodology to identify clusters based on the density of data points. It distinguishes core points that possess numerous neighbors within a predetermined distance, subsequently expanding clusters from these cores. Furthermore, it can label isolated points as noise. This approach proves particularly effective in identifying clusters of irregular shapes and detecting outliers.

The third approach, **Hierarchical Clustering**, builds a tree-like structure of clusters, either by starting with each point as its own cluster and merging them (agglomerative approach) or by starting with one large cluster and dividing it (divisive approach). This method provides a detailed view of how data points relate to each other at different levels of granularity, allowing one to choose the most appropriate number of clusters after seeing the full hierarchy.

The selection of clustering algorithms depends on the specific requirements. K-means is suitable when the number of clusters is known and expected to be approximately circular. DBSCAN is appropriate for handling irregular shapes and noise. Hierarchical clustering is preferred when understanding the relationships between clusters at various scales is the primary objective.

If the object does not belong to any cluster, it is definitely an outlier. It is an outlier if the object and the closest clusters have a large distance. If the object is part of a small and sparse cluster, then all objects in this small cluster are outliers. In any case, significant domain expertise is required to determine if the outliers are errors. In this case, they can be ignored or tracked as a quantity of error in the dataset. However, if the outliers are identified as an important anomaly of the dataset, they have to be evaluated properly.

Smoothing Noisy Data

Real-world datasets often contain noise—random variations or inaccuracies that can obscure underlying patterns and relationships. Smoothing noisy data is a crucial preprocessing step that helps to reduce these irregularities and enhance the signal-to-noise ratio. Following techniques for smoothing noisy data:

- **Binning**. This is as well-known as bucketing. It sorts data into groups "bins" chosen based on their values. It is particularly useful for handling noisy data by reducing the effects of minor observation errors. Localized fluctuations are better represented by grouping neighboring data points, and the overall trend enhances visibility. The binning process requires the data to be sorted first in ascending or descending order. The next step is to divide the sorted data into a specific number of bins. As necessary, the bins may be smoothed by replacing the values with the mean, median, and closest boundary value. This is a fast approach that is easy to implement and very effective in eliminating minor observation error values. It is also applicable to numerical and categorical values. The process needs careful consideration and adjustment. The chosen bin size will significantly affect the results, with the wrong size and number of bins causing a loss of information.

- **Regression**. Regression is a very reliable approach to modeling relationships between variables. To smooth noisy data, regression techniques fit the data to a function, effectively creating a "best fit" line or curves. This represents the overall trend while minimizing the impact of noise.

- **Linear regression**. Linear regression will fit the data to a straight line. Polynomial regression uses higher-degree polynomials to represent complex relationships in the data, and local regression fits multiple regressions in local neighborhoods. Regression algorithms capture underlying trends effectively and provide mathematical models of the relationships. They are very flexible and use many types of regression to cover different data patterns. Like any algorithm, it requires careful review as regression algorithms expect specific forms or relationships between the variables. Over-smoothing and missing important local variations can easily be created and miss the goal. Linear regression is very sensitive to outliers.

CHAPTER FOUR

Data Mining

Political Background—Afghanistan

The September 11, 2001 terrorist attacks on the US, orchestrated by al-Qaeda from Afghanistan, led to an immediate international response. When the Taliban refused to extradite bin Laden, the US, with NATO allies, launched Operation Enduring Freedom on October 7, 2001.

Following the defeat of the Taliban and the signing of an international agreement to establish a functioning government, the reconstruction effort encountered numerous obstacles. Decades of conflict had severely damaged much of Afghanistan's infrastructure and institutions. The country's economy was heavily dependent on opium production, which proved challenging to replace with viable alternatives.

Despite these challenges, Afghanistan was established as an Islamic republic with a robust presidential system in January 2004, while safeguarding fundamental rights, including women's rights and religious freedoms.

The inaugural presidential election in Afghan history was scheduled for October 9, 2004, which was accompanied by severe threats from the remaining forces of the Taliban.

The task assigned to the US army was to develop a sophisticated tool to comprehend the movement of Taliban forces based on signals intelligence (SIGINT) and human intelligence (HUMINT), with a new, sophisticated analysis and prediction engine.

Iraq War and Occupation (2002-2007)

The Iraq War commenced with the invasion in March 2003, resulting in the defeat of Saddam Hussein's army and the occupation of Baghdad in April of the same year.

The Coalition Provisional Authority encountered significant and unforeseen consequences. A substantial number of unemployed and armed individuals from the defeated army formed dispersed groups throughout the country, establishing the foundation of insurgency. Several insurgent groups emerged, garnering support from disenfranchised segments of the population. Sectarian tensions between Sunni and Shia populations escalated, while anti-occupation sentiment surged among a broad spectrum of Iraqi society.

The equipment developed during the Afghanistan War required substantial extensions to comprehend the diverse streams of development in Iraq and anticipate unforeseen events. These initially manifested as attacks by insurgent groups and the construction of improvised explosive devices of various sizes.

At this juncture, it became imperative to identify any means that could disrupt coalition operations. Human intelligence (HUMINT) remained a crucial component, but signal intelligence (SIGINT) gained greater significance in comprehending financial transactions, material movements, and equipment procurement.

Patented State of the Art Engine

The tooling and the outline of the machine learning algorithms were meticulously designed by the author of this book and subsequently refined during the implementation process. This was achieved through the collaborative efforts of a team of experts with extensive expertise in the relevant domain. The development process was iterative, guided, and continually updated in response to the feedback received from challenges encountered.

The design was successfully deployed and validated in Afghanistan and Iraq. The high-level goals were defined as:

- Fully distributed Big Data infrastructure with decentralized persistence and predictive analytics.

- Constant bidirectional synchronization protecting clearance levels at every node: secret, top secret, and higher TS-SCI.

- All local points down to laptops and mobile devices applied machine learning algorithms against the last synchronized device data set.

- Complex events were dynamically reduced down to atomic correlations based on single attributes.

- Automated algorithmic analysis of all relevant attributes were performed and taken together over time to define the progression of the set of interrelated events.

- High-performance parallel processing, was conducted to eliminate noise from the data stream to create the operational dataset.

- Microscopic time-based pattern grids of the environment were extracted and adjustments applied as new input arrived in the data stream.

The design, which was employed nearly two decades ago, used state-of-the-art technology and played a pivotal role in mitigating potentially catastrophic events during and after the Afghanistan and Iraq wars.

Let's explore the challenges and the high-level operation flow of the framework.

Improvised Electronic Devices (IEDs) were strategically placed to disrupt the control and implementation of safe zones. These devices could be activated partially through cell phones or manually.

The complexity was in the fact that the individuals responsible for these operations were not affiliated with large-scale organizations. They were often lone individuals tasked with posting or activating the devices without a centralized background for a small change. The overall coordination was orchestrated by organizations that remained concealed from the public view.

To cause significant damage through an explosion, materials must be transported to the target location and purchased, which requires substantial monetary resources. Money was usually broken down into chunks and used in various ways to reach the target to avoid tracking.

The operations were conducted by small, isolated cells—terrorist or organized Taliban members to avoid traceability.

If cell A collaborated with cell B, communication between their leaders had to be avoided. Therefore, information had to flow through low-level cell members. The inference engine was required to trace deep-nested links to identify the link between cell A and cell B.

Conventional physical modeling frameworks have demonstrated efficacy in predicting outcomes for simple, causally linked events where variables exhibit established patterns. However, this approach was inadequate in addressing the dynamic nature of criminal and terrorist organizations, which deliberately employed adaptive and opportunistic strategies to evade detection and prediction. These adversarial entities systematically modified their tactical procedures, operational patterns, and organizational structures to undermine traditional predictive models.

The adversaries' capacity for rapid tactical evolution and intentional efforts to conceal their activities pose substantial challenges to conventional analysis methodologies. They frequently modify their communication channels, financial transactions, and operational signatures, while simultaneously introducing deliberate noise and false patterns to evade detection systems. This adaptive behavior renders traditional physical modeling approaches increasingly unreliable for threat prediction and prevention.

To address these challenges, a more sophisticated system and methodology were required—one capable of identifying and analyzing obfuscated relationships embedded within large-scale, complex datasets. Such a system needed to detect subtle patterns, indirect connections, and emergent behaviors that signify potential future activities, while accounting for the adversaries' deliberate attempts at deception and pattern disruption. The solution demanded advanced capabilities in processing multi-dimensional data relationships, identifying non-obvious correlations, and adapting to evolving adversarial tactics in real time.

The "Mining Engine and Prediction Background" section explains how this data analysis framework worked in real-world scenarios, such as detecting explosive devices in urban areas, sparsely populated places, or difficult-to-reach terrains. Developed two decades ago, this approach used any available technology to preemptively detect and track such activities, preventing potential events.

Operation

We now delve into the distributed analysis system's architecture and components, focusing on data processing, storage, and analysis across multiple nodes and locations. Unlike traditional analysis systems, it operated on historical activities and future pattern predictions in parallel, enabling proactive insight generation.

The distributed analysis system's foundation was its persistent store, the primary data repository. This infrastructure provides:

- Data Injection Capabilities require real-time data ingestion from multiple sources.

- Support for various data formats and structures with buffering mechanisms for high-volume data streams and quality control and validation checks needed to be implemented.

- Seamless interaction with cloud and remote resources were needed, as well as distributed result retrieval and storage mechanisms with load balancing across the instances.

- Resource optimization algorithms were also required.

Structured Metadata organized hierarchically with reliable version control and change tracking across distributed instances are required, as well as fast relationship mapping between metadata elements. Obviously, the system was not useful without high performance and advanced search and retrieval capabilities.

Data was collected from various structured and unstructured sources and transformed into structured metadata of objects (entities) and attributes. This metadata encompassed detailed content information, precise geo-location, and time.

Entities were the fundamental processing units that contained attributes. These were the basic elements defined and, if necessary, extended by trained analysts to meet the operational requirements of the space. The analyst could add hints to relationship mapping, validation rules, and conflict resolution. Version control for some entities was helpful to backtrack obfuscated objects (entities).

Attributes were specific data associated with entities. Trained analysts could define, modify, or extend relevant attributes for each entity and flag one or a few attributes as important for correlation. This enabled attributes of one entity to be mapped to attributes in other entities, regardless of their labels.

The data input had a flexible entity definition system that allowed for the modification and creation of custom attributes. The analyst could add hints for relationship mapping, validation rules, and conflict resolution. Version control for some entities was helpful to backtrack obfuscated objects (entities). This enabled attributes of one entity to map to attributes in other entities, regardless of their labels.

The analyst could adjust the system's front-end input to parse incoming data and filter it based on specific attributes of an entity. For instance, the analyst could focus on financial transfers exceeding $10,000.

As the analytic engine processed the data, it first identified micro-patterns in the data and created a dependency graph of these objects. A micro-pattern captures the behavior of micro-level relationships that are discovered during correlation processing.

The inference engine started to analyze the collection of super-objects, compared data values of the super-objects and established relationships across the relevant data using the micro-pattern graph.

The machine learning path used an iterative process where the algorithm constantly identified relationships in the data. It learned how features (attributes) correlate to each other in the selected data set. The algorithm adjusted its internal weights and parameters based on the differences between its predictions and actual values, gradually improving its accuracy through many iterations of this process.

Model optimization happened by iterative evaluation or the complexity of the decision boundaries in tree-based models. The used architecture balanced complexity (to capture intricate patterns) with simplicity (to avoid overfitting) and was refined through empirical testing and domain expertise.

The result of this operation generated events from the collected data. These were extremely important steps to create the ground-truth of events.

An event was characterized by a temporal reference and, optionally, a geospatial location reference. These references may have been associated with one or more entities or super-objects. The "name" or "label" assigned to events in this approach would automatically be assigned during the process. The analyst also had the option to accept or manually refine.

Like the event creation mechanism, the inference created multiple super-objects or none, depending on the number of distinct correlations common among different entities. In addition, the process correlated entities that are part of an event.

The super-object was a tree-like structure containing all the correlated entities discovered during the data correlation process, including associated events with a time and location reference.

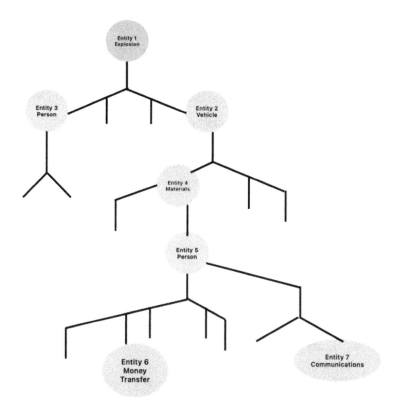

The example explosion event entity was the "vertex" with the most related "edges" in the super-object. For visualization, it could be shown as a tree structure or displayed as a geographic map of all types of entities.

The inference engine operated on micro-patterns and provided awareness of discovered relationships through composite network representations and, if required, visualization. The micro-patterns were generated on the simplest two-node pattern. Predicting future events was calculated by predicting the activity of these two-node patterns.

The advantage of micro-pattern operations over physical models or systems that rely on larger patterns for operation is that the prediction capabilities of the system and method of this approach are not fooled by an event that occurs out of sequence, such as a change in tactics used previously or by an act of deception.

The flow of functional processing was broken down into six major components:

- Configuration
- Metadata generation
- Data conditioning
- Correlation and reduction
- Prediction
- Learning loop.

After the collected source data has been processed by the data mapper and translated to standard processing objects, the objects were processed by the process engine or user-defined data filters and stored in a metadata repository before entering the data correlation and prediction framework.

The metadata generated by the data mapper included all events and entities, including their associated attributes found in the collected source data (e.g., input data). The metadata output of the data mapper that successfully passed through the defined data filters was stored in the metadata repository. The metadata repository was the persistent store for the output of the data mapper and data filters.

In the data conditioning processing phase, the inference engine primarily executed a data conditioning/cleansing operation to fill in missing values within a context.

Subsequently, the analysis performed reduction, consolidation, and correlation on the event and entity metadata. The following page provides a high-level overview of the flow and a detailed description of the analytic steps.

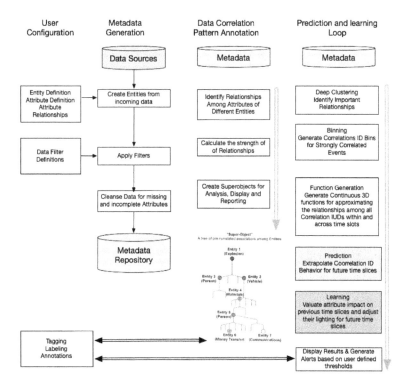

The picture above shows the entire flow: user adjustment of the configuration, creation of the metadata, and creation of micro-patterns to super-objects. Data validation, cleansing, and continuous prediction happened, as well as the feedback from the learning to extend the metadata from new data feeds.

During the inference process, data validation and cleansing encompassed several crucial processes. Firstly, the algorithm identified missing values by systematically examining each data column. It subsequently detected patterns within the gaps and employed techniques, such as mean/median imputation, forward/backward filling for time series, or more sophisticated methods like k-nearest neighbors to address these gaps.

The algorithm then detected outliers using statistical methods like z-scores, IQR ranges, or isolation forests. These anomalous values were either removed, capped at threshold values, or transformed to maintain data integrity while preventing them from skewing the model.

Data type consistency was enforced by converting mismatched formats, standardizing date/time representations, and ensuring numerical fields contained only valid numbers. Text fields were standardized through case normalization, special character removal, and consistent formatting.

Feature scaling followed, where numerical values were normalized or standardized to similar ranges, typically 0-1 or having zero mean and unit variance. This ensured all features contribute proportionally to the model's learning process.

Duplicate records were identified and removed based on exact matches or similarity thresholds, preserving data quality while preventing the over representation of certain patterns. This was an iterative process followed by discovering all correlations that existed between different entities in the metadata.

The identification of relationships among attributes of different entities is followed by calculating the strength of the relationships. Generating a super-object was a significant part of the inference engine used for reporting and display. An example of a simple network appears here:

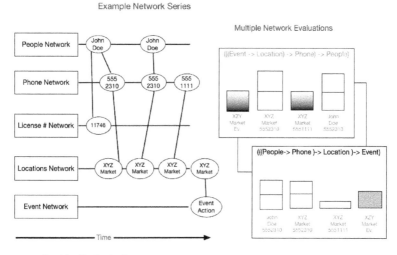

The analysis quantified relationship strengths through spatiotemporal and content-based distance metrics. The correlation methodology employed multivariate statistical techniques to identify significant relationships and assess their statistical relevance.

We were not using the Euclidean distance, which is a straightforward and commonly used way to measure the distance between two points in space, based on the Pythagorean theorem. It calculates the straight-line distance by taking the square root of the sum of the squared differences between corresponding coordinates.

In our case, to identify outliers in multivariate data, the algorithm utilized the Mahalanobis distance, a measure of the number of standard deviations a data point deviates from the mean of the distribution. Unlike the Euclidean distance, the Mahalanobis distance took into account the correlations between variables and was unaffected by the scale of different measurements. It calculated the distance between each point and the center of the data distribution while considering the shape (covariance) of the data. For instance, in a dataset containing both height and weight measurements, the Mahalanobis distance would recognize that these variables are naturally correlated and would identify outliers based on the unusualness of their combination rather than solely examining each measurement separately.

The formula:

$$(D^2(x) = (x - \mu)^T \Sigma^{-1} (x - \mu))$$

calculated this distance by first finding how far a point is from the average $(x - \mu)$. It then adjusts how variables interact with each other.

In the next step, a single number was produced, marking how unusual that point is. To handle cases where some patterns appeared very rarely in the data, the system used a special weighting approach. It provided more importance to rare patterns using this formula:

$$w(e) = \log(N/f(e))$$

This is how search engines give more weight to rare words. If something happens very infrequently, it might be more significant when it does occur. This balanced approach ensured that important but rare patterns weren't overshadowed by common ones while maintaining statistical reliability.

This weighting scheme ensured that low-frequency entities maintained appropriate statistical significance in the correlation analysis, preventing bias towards high-frequency observations while preserving the statistical validity of the relationship strength measurements.

The networks generated during correlation processing were created at an atomic level, resulting in a high number and complexity of network sequences that became challenging to manage for both the system and the user. To address this issue, the correlation process of the engine continuously created vertices and weighted edges on the network sequences and then iteratively "pan-caked" (i.e., collapsed) the networks. An illustration of the iterative "pancaking" process performed between different network layers to collapse correlations down to a correlated network sequence, or "super-object," is shown below.

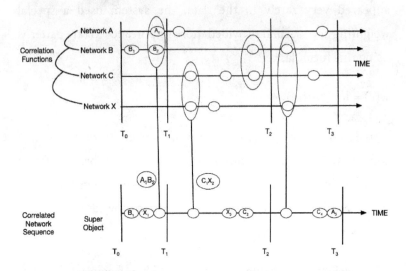

While the super-object depicted the simplified representation of the processed data, it was crucial to understand that processed metadata stayed retained in the metadata repository to provide a drill-down capability for the user in the presentation of the results and to facilitate future processing when new collected source data was received.

The results of the correlation processing were presented to the analyst user either as a *Nodal Graph View* presenting all correlated entities and their relationships, or as a *Time Series View* that helped to understand the evolution of the network over time.

The framework in operation applied a prediction algorithm to the relationships between entities over time. Using past and present collected source data, the prediction algorithm dynamically generated estimated "future data" along with associated error margins. A prerequisite to generating valid, future predictions, was that there was an adequate volume of interrelated input collected source data to generate enough correlations.

The algorithm predicted the magnitude of the next correlations from the generated information and functions with a time extrapolation. Operating in sequence, it created the set of super-objects injected into the prediction algorithm using correlation. A deep clustering approach determined the relevance of important relationships from the source data.

From the set of identified important relationships, the prediction algorithm of the inference engine generated time-dependent correlation bins that contained occurrences of specific attributes from the event data.

Alarms and recommendations were derived from sequential operations based on predefined thresholds. The results were consolidated into a graphical representation for decision-making.

The following paragraph provides an overview of the prediction algorithm's theoretical underpinnings.

Identification of Correlated Entities

The correlation bins were generated exclusively for entities identified as correlated during the deep clustering process. The deep clustering process determined the strength of the relationships based on the attribute types and the distribution functions.

In the deep clustering process, several complementary distance and similarity measures were employed to accommodate diverse data attributes. The Minkowski distance was used for numerical data, which serves as a generalization of both Euclidean and Manhattan distances. It is calculated as the nth root of the sum of the absolute differences between coordinates raised to the power n. When n equals 2, it reduces to the conventional Euclidean distance, while when n equals 1, it transforms into the Manhattan distance.

For binary attributes (data with yes/no or 0/1 values), specialized binary distance measures have been implemented. These measures quantified the number of matching and non-matching pairs of attributes between two objects, taking into account the relative significance of the presence or absence of a feature in the context of the specific analysis.

To measure the similarity between sets of data, two additional coefficients were employed: the Extended Jaccard similarity coefficient and the Dice coefficient. The Extended Jaccard similarity coefficient calculates the ratio of the intersection of two sets to their union, while accounting for the magnitude of numeric values. This makes it suitable for non-binary data. The Dice coefficient, like Jaccard, gives more weight to agreements between sets by calculating twice the number of common terms divided by the total number of terms in both sets. These similarity measures are particularly useful when comparing documents, genetic sequences, or other data where the overlap between sets is more important than the absolute distances between values.

Once the strength of the dependencies among entities has been determined, software containers for correlations of a specific type could be created as containers, including the relationship of the entity points to its parent event.

In the overall process, a flow of operations upon incoming collected source data was performed to consolidate using the embedded filtering. Every time the processes worked on incoming data, new elements of the same type of correlation were added to the bin, along with their associated time.

The progression of events over time was captured through the analysis of all the bins collectively. Functionally, the significance of the bins was to reduce a set of complex events to create atomic correlations on a single attribute. When prediction algorithms were applied to these atomic correlations, the prediction algorithms were self-controlled.

The transitions restricted to a single bin were fast, and the results could easily be validated, yet they remained highly effective because they impacted the entire data set.

For simplicity, the magnitude of each bin in each time slice, which was viewed as a data point representing the peak of each bin on the vertical axis, was defined. Once a network segment of finite nodes was established, the source and destination of a movement stayed static as long as the path of traversed nodes with an average service time was less than or equal to the average service time of the network layer. The base model for a single network layer was a queueing network.

The system used a technique called a multivariate Markov chain to understand how different sequences of events influenced each other over time. The assumption was that tracking multiple parallel storylines and predicting how each one would develop was based on what happened in all the others.

For instance, if monitoring multiple suspicious activities, the observation showed that money transfers between a network of various accounts may appear independent. However, communications related to each other are not visible on the surface. It is only possible to identify them by analyzing deeply nested relationships, which would turn these independent events into one coordinated event.

Independent travel movements are only clustered by the target goal as well as supply chain activities, small to large, or composed at the end of all independent activities. The model looked at how these different activities affect each other. If we saw pattern A in money transfers, pattern B in communications, and pattern C in travel, what was likely to happen next in each of these areas?

The mathematical formula:

$$P(X_i, t+1 \mid X_1, t...s, t, X_1, t-1...s, t-1, ..., X_1, t-n+1...s, t-n+1)$$

showed the probability of the next event in sequence i, given what was observed in all sequences over the last n time periods.

The challenge with this approach was that it became extremely complex very quickly. Each additional piece of history is multiplied by the number of possibilities needed to track. Raftery[2] (1985) developed a simpler method that made the calculations more manageable while maintaining accuracy.

This approach was particularly useful for detecting coordinated activities across different domains and predicting how changes in one area would affect others.

> *Complex patterns could be identified, not visible when looking at each sequence in isolation.*

More importantly, it enabled the finding of hidden connections between seemingly unrelated events.

The distributed analysis used the aforementioned theory to determine the magnitudes of each bin in each time slice. Though actual data was available for all time slices, the process predicted bins for each time slice to compare to actual data and improve error margins.

---

[2] Raftery, A. (1985) A Model for Higher Order Markov Chains, Journal of Royal Statistical Society, Series B, 47:528-539).

Performance optimization is crucial in data mining and prediction development. This approach prioritized design decisions within software modules to enhance the overall system's performance. While accurate functionality was essential, all software modules also needed to enable high performance when implemented as a geographically distributed system.

Key design considerations to achieve high performance included:

- **Parallel Processing.** The complexity and impact of the data input architecture made sense to have a single component, which could be load-based distributed to achieve the desired performance by the application control over every task in a parallelized environment. As the large data set could not be automatically segmented, an enhanced algorithmic approach created a dependency graph of segments process isolated and synchronized to avoid any data or correlation loss. This allowed tasks to be distributed according to the running algorithm that do not depend on the kernel scheduler.

- **Fully Distributed Analysis System with Dynamic Synchronization of All Outputs.** The process operated with near-real-time performance in a geographically dispersed environment, continuously processing incoming collected data and constantly synchronizing its distributed output across the entire system. This fully distributed, fully synchronized mining, correlation, and prediction capability represented a substantial advancement over current state-of-the-art systems at the time.

Time and space complexity considerations were used to adjust the processing unit. To optimize the process capability, precise measurements were taken for data ingestion, pattern recognition, prediction generation, clustering operations, in-memory processing limits, and the available network bandwidth. The result of these measurements was used to iteratively optimize the processing engine. There were also methods implemented to adjust during the operation without compromising the quality.

Predictive Deployment in Afghanistan

This processing structure was employed on secure mobile devices to monitor the movement of hostile forces (red forces) in the months preceding the first election in Afghanistan. The utilized data in this instance consisted of some sensible Department of Defense (DoD) data, but more infrastructure information pertaining to people's available resources, such as electricity, water, and education facilities. Additionally, data about the education levels of the population was collected from various non-governmental organizations (NGOs).

The data was processed and predictions were made regarding the movement of hostile forces and subsequent violence in various regions of the country. Based on these predictions, Blue Forces were deployed to secure the access and security of the population during the election.

The predictive capabilities in the environment were precisely validated after the election, demonstrating the efficiency of the inference engine, which ranged between 85-95%.

The LLM Approach

The pure ML approach can be extended to leverage Large Language Models (LLMs) and GANs (Generative Adversary Networks) as the available data will be unlabeled.

Below, we delve into the groundbreaking application of LLMs and GANs in scientific research, with a specific focus on their capabilities in extracting and analyzing unlabeled data. We explore how these technologies are revolutionizing research methodologies across diverse scientific disciplines, thereby opening up novel avenues for scientific discovery.

The exponential growth of available data has presented both opportunities and challenges for researchers. While the volume of data has increased significantly, the traditional bottleneck of manual data annotation and analysis has become more pronounced. LLMs and GANs have emerged as potent tools to address these challenges, offering innovative approaches to unlock insights from unlabeled scientific data.

LLMs significantly contribute to the equation by processing the vast amounts of scientific literature available. They enable the automated extraction of key findings and methodologies, identification of research gaps and emerging trends, and discovery of cross-disciplinary connections. LLMs also facilitate hypothesis generation based on existing literature.

LLMs exhibit remarkable abilities in pattern recognition across diverse datasets, anomaly detection in experimental results, context-aware interpretation of scientific data, and natural language interfaces for complex queries.

GANs in the Scientific Data Processing

Generative Adversarial Networks (GANs)

GANs represent a pretty new framework in machine learning, introduced by Ian Goodfellow and colleagues in 2014. This framework consists of two neural networks competing against each other in a minimax game, generating highly realistic synthetic data. The generator is the network that creates the data, and the discriminator network is a classifier that specializes in distinguishing real data from the generated data. Each network is trained independently.

Core Architecture

Generator Network (G)

The generator network, a fundamental component of the Generative Adversarial Network (GAN) framework, plays a pivotal role in the creative process. Its primary functions encompass:

- Transforming random noise vectors into synthetic data samples
- Learning the underlying distribution of the training data
- Mapping from a latent space (Z) to the desired data space (X)
- Continuously enhancing output quality through iterative feedback from the discriminator.

Discriminator Network (D)

The discriminator functions as a binary classifier with the following characteristics:

- Evaluates both real and generated samples
- Outputs probability scores indicating the authenticity of each sample
- Provides gradient feedback to the generator

- Maps from the data space X to the probability space [0,1].

The training process involves discriminator optimization by maximizing the ability to distinguish real from fake samples and by updating weights to minimize classification errors. The generator optimization minimizes the probability of detection by the discriminator and updates weights to produce more convincing samples.

Concepts Beyond the Basics

GANs have shown significant research benefits over the past decade, yet core issues of training instability and mode collapse persist. Work is in progress with SwarmGAN, a novel GAN framework incorporating swarm intelligence to address these limitations. Specifically, swarm intelligence exhibits properties well-suited to enhance GAN training: emergent complex behaviors arising from simple individual agents, decentralized adaptability to instantaneous data and hyperparameters, and robustness through simple iterative interactions. SwarmGAN incorporates a particle swarm optimization algorithm to guide the generator and discriminator updates.

The system's performance could be enhanced by employing convolutional neural networks (CNNs), specialized deep learning architectures that excel at processing visual data by applying filters to identify patterns and features at various scales. Gradient penalties were implemented to ensure stable training by mitigating extreme gradient values that could lead to training collapse.

The effectiveness of the system was rigorously evaluated using several key metrics:

Fréchet Inception Distance (FID): This metric assesses the similarity between generated images and real-world counterparts by comparing their feature distributions. Lower scores denote more realistic outputs.

Inception Score (IS): This evaluation assesses both the quality and diversity of generated images by measuring the degree of confidence with which they can be classified into distinct categories while maintaining consistency within those categories.

Peak Signal-to-Noise Ratio (PSNR): This metric compares the maximum possible signal power to the corrupting noise power, helping assess the quality of image reconstruction.

Structural Similarity Index Score (SSIM): This evaluation assesses the perceived quality of digital images and videos by quantifying the structural similarity between the original and generated images. Factors such as luminance, contrast, and structure are taken into account during this comparison.

These comprehensive evaluations revealed enhancements in three pivotal areas: training stability (the consistency and reliability of the model's behavior), sample quality (the realism and clarity of the generated images), and convergence speed (the rate at which the model attains optimal performance). Integrating swarm optimization techniques with generative adversarial networks (GANs) demonstrated particular promise in addressing prevalent challenges associated with GAN training, including mode collapse and training instability.

Still, remaining challenges are listed below:

There are several loss function variants.

1. Original GAN Loss:
   a. Based on binary cross-entropy
   b. Prone to vanishing gradients
   c. Suitable for simple applications.

2. Wasserstein Loss:
   a. Provides more stable gradients
   b. Better convergence properties
   c. Requires weight clipping or gradient penalty.

3. Least Squares Loss:
   a. Reduces vanishing gradient problems
   b. More stable training dynamics
   c. Improved sample quality.

GANs provide significant benefits in analyzing data with competing networks, but the challenges they create are also significant.

The generator may produce significantly limited variety potential. Addressing approaches include mini-batch discrimination and regularization of diversity promotion.

Several techniques can assist in stabilizing the training process of neural networks. Gradient penalty functions mitigate extreme gradient values that could disrupt training. Spectral normalization regulates the network's layer weights, ensuring smoother training dynamics. The Two-timescale Update Rule (TTUR) employs distinct learning rates for the generator and discriminator networks. Typically, the discriminator receives a slower learning rate compared to the generator. This differential learning pace facilitates the establishment of equilibrium between the two networks during training, preventing either from becoming excessively dominant and overwhelming the other.

In the context of generative adversarial networks (GANs), the training process resembles a game where one player, the generator, attempts to create convincing fake images, while the other player, the discriminator, endeavors to identify these fakes. If the generator gains an advantage too quickly, it may dominate the process, leaving the discriminator with insufficient time to enhance its skills. Conversely, by allowing the discriminator to learn at a slower pace, both players can simultaneously improve their abilities.

While these methods show promise in theory, their effectiveness needs to be carefully tested across different scenarios and datasets to understand their practical benefits and limitations.

A generic implementation adheres to best practices as architectural guidelines for network design. Key considerations include employing transposed convolutions for up-sampling. Batch normalization requires careful implementation and evaluation. Additionally, appropriate stride and padding along leaky ReLU activation should be taken into account.

The training strategy should precisely follow these steps for data processing to reduce the challenges by normalizing inputs to [-1, 1] range. It then applies data augmentation when appropriate to ensure consistency and handle missing or corrupt data. Monitoring and evaluating the track loss convergence and sample diversity is necessary. It has to calculate FID scores and assess inception scores.

GANs can significantly augment the data by generating training data, class balancing, and very important rare event simulations to support the outlined mining process.

Despite the numerous constraints, Generative Adversarial Networks (GANs) remain a robust framework for generative modeling, finding widespread applications across diverse domains. While training and architecture design challenges persist, ongoing advancements in loss functions, regularization techniques, and architectural innovations have rendered GANs increasingly practical and effective. As research progresses, GANs are anticipated to assume a progressively pivotal role in artificial intelligence and machine learning applications.

The success of Generative Adversarial Networks (GANs) hinges on meticulous consideration of architecture design, loss function selection, and training methodologies. A thorough comprehension of these technical aspects is paramount for developing effective GAN-based solutions and propelling the field forward.

The combination of LLMs and GANs represents a promising scientific research space with the potential to develop an extremely effective toolkit. While challenges remain, the potential for accelerating discovery and gaining deeper insights from unlabeled data makes these technologies invaluable for the scientific community. Continued development and refinement of these approaches will likely lead to even more powerful research tools in the future.

CHAPTER FIVE

Key Findings

As we reflect on the evolution of data collection and analysis in hostile environments, a clear picture emerges of both remarkable progress and persistent challenges. The past decade has witnessed a transformation in how organizations approach data gathering and analysis under adverse conditions, yielding valuable insights that continue to shape the field.

Integrating multiple data streams has emerged as perhaps the most critical advancement in hostile environment data science. Organizations have learned to effectively combine traditional field observations with automated sensor data, creating rich, multi-layered datasets that provide unprecedented insight into complex situations. This integration, however, has not been without its challenges. Teams have had to develop sophisticated approaches to harmonizing data from disparate sources, each with its own temporal and spatial scales, quality parameters, and reliability considerations.

The success of these integration efforts has largely depended on the development of standardized data formats and protocols that can accommodate diverse data types while maintaining stringent quality standards. Organizations that have excelled in this area have typically invested heavily in developing flexible data models and robust validation systems that can handle the complexity of multi-modal data streams while ensuring data integrity.

Experience has demonstrated that adaptive collection strategies are indispensable for success in challenging environments. Rather than rigid protocols, successful organizations have implemented adaptable methodologies that can swiftly adjust to evolving conditions. This adaptive approach extends beyond mere data collection to encompass risk management, resource allocation, and safety protocols. Teams have honed their operational effectiveness while ensuring personnel safety through continuous threat assessment and dynamic response protocols.

Critical Success Factors

Several key factors have consistently emerged as essential for successful operations in hostile environments. At the technical level, the reliability and resilience of equipment have proven crucial. Organizations have learned that investing in robust hardware and redundant systems yields dividends in terms of data quality and operational continuity. However, technical excellence alone is insufficient.

Operational effectiveness also hinges on well-trained and adaptable personnel who can make informed decisions under pressure. The human element remains paramount to successful data collection in hostile environments, with strong local partnerships often proving as valuable as advanced technology. Organizations that have invested in comprehensive training programs and established robust relationships with local communities have consistently achieved superior results compared to those relying solely on technical solutions.

The organizational framework supporting these operations has proven equally important. Strong leadership commitment, clear governance structures, and effective knowledge management systems have emerged as common features of successful programs. Organizations that maintain flexible resource allocation systems and embrace continuous improvement processes demonstrate greater resilience in the face of evolving challenges.

Emerging Development in Technologies

The field of hostile environment data science is experiencing rapid evolution, propelled by technological advancements and evolving operational demands. Several key trends are shaping the future of this discipline, with artificial intelligence (AI) and machine learning (ML) emerging as pivotal drivers.

Integrating AI and ML into hostile environment operations has transcended simple automation, encompassing sophisticated decision support systems and predictive analytics. Contemporary AI systems can perform real-time threat assessment, optimize collection strategies, and validate data quality autonomously. These capabilities have revolutionized how organizations approach data acquisition in challenging environments.

Autonomous systems have attained remarkable sophistication, incorporating advanced decision-making capabilities that can adapt to changing conditions without human intervention. Smart sensor networks can now autonomously adjust their collection parameters based on environmental factors, threat levels, and data quality requirements. This autonomy has proven particularly valuable in environments where human access is restricted or hazardous.

The evolution of predictive analytics has enabled organizations to anticipate and prepare for potential challenges before they materialize. Modern systems can analyze intricate patterns in historical data to forecast potential risks and optimize resource allocation. This predictive capability has proven particularly valuable in dynamic environments where conditions can change rapidly.

Distributed Intelligence

The emergence of edge computing has revolutionized data collection in hostile environments by enabling sophisticated processing capabilities at the point of collection. This distributed approach has reduced reliance on central processing systems and minimized data transmission requirements, making operations more resilient to communication disruptions.

Smart sensor networks have evolved to incorporate sophisticated edge processing capabilities, enabling real-time analysis and decision-making at the collection point. These networks can now self-organize, automatically adjust their collection strategies, and collaborate to validate data quality. The ability to process data locally has reduced bandwidth requirements and improved system resilience, while enabling more rapid response to changing conditions.

Implementing distributed intelligence has created new possibilities for resilient operations in hostile environments. Mesh networks can now maintain connectivity even when individual nodes fail, while distributed storage solutions ensure data preservation under adverse conditions. These advances have significantly improved the reliability of data collection operations in challenging environments.

Quantum Computing Impact

The emergence of quantum computing presents both opportunities and challenges for hostile environment data science. While still in its early stages, quantum computing promises to revolutionize certain data processing and security aspects. The potential for solving complex optimization problems and enhancing cryptographic security is particularly relevant to operations in hostile environments.

However, the implementation of quantum computing solutions presents significant challenges. The specialized hardware requirements, high costs, and complexity of quantum systems make their widespread deployment in hostile environments unlikely in the near term. Nevertheless, organizations are beginning to explore hybrid approaches that combine classical and quantum computing capabilities to enhance specific aspects of their operations.

Blockchain and Secure Data Collection

Blockchain technology has emerged as a powerful tool for ensuring data integrity and maintaining secure chains of custody in hostile environments. The technology's ability to create immutable records and provide transparent audit trails has proven particularly valuable when data authenticity is crucial.

The implementation of smart contracts has automated many aspects of data sharing and access control, reducing administrative overhead while improving security. Organizations have found particular value in blockchain's ability to automate compliance tracking and validate data provenance, though challenges remain in terms of scalability and resource requirements.

The integration of blockchain technology with existing data collection systems requires careful consideration of technical and operational factors. Organizations must balance the benefits of enhanced security and transparency against the computational overhead and complexity introduced by blockchain systems. Successful implementations typically take an incremental approach, starting with critical data streams and gradually expanding coverage as expertise and infrastructure develop.

Additional Challenges and Opportunities

The landscape of data collection and analysis in hostile environments continues to evolve, presenting both new challenges and unprecedented opportunities. As we look to the future, several key areas demand particular attention from practitioners and researchers alike.

Migration and Evolution of Hostile Environments

The nature of hostile environments is undergoing a rapid transformation driven by technological advancements, climate change, and geopolitical shifts. Traditional physical access and safety challenges are compounded by increasingly sophisticated digital threats and complex regulatory environments. Organizations must now prepare for hybrid threats that combine physical, digital, and social elements in ways that can be difficult to predict or counter.

Climate change has emerged as a particular concern, creating new types of hostile environments and exacerbating existing challenges. Extreme weather events, changing environmental conditions, and infrastructure degradation create new obstacles to data collection while simultaneously increasing the demand for reliable environmental data. Organizations must develop more resilient collection systems while preparing for conditions that may have no historical precedent.

The increasing interconnectedness of global systems has created new vulnerabilities while offering new data collection opportunities. Digital networks spanning traditional boundaries can provide valuable data streams and attractive targets for adversaries. Organizations must balance the benefits of connectivity against the risks of exposure and compromise.

Technological Challenges

The rapid pace of technological advancement presents its own set of challenges. While new technologies offer potent capabilities, they also introduce complexities in terms of integration, maintenance, and security. Organizations must meticulously assess new technologies not only for their immediate benefits but also for their long-term sustainability in hostile environments.

The proliferation of sensors and data collection devices has engendered data management and integration challenges. Organizations must devise novel approaches to handle the voluminous, diverse, and rapid influx of data while ensuring its quality and relevance. The challenge of maintaining and calibrating increasingly intricate sensor networks in hostile environments necessitates innovative system design and maintenance strategies.

Power management has emerged as a paramount concern, particularly for remote and autonomous systems. The development of more energy-efficient systems and reliable power sources remains a key challenge, especially in environments where conventional power infrastructure is unreliable or nonexistent.

Drawing upon accumulated experience and emerging trends, several salient recommendations emerge for organizations operating in hostile environments.

Framework for Sustainable Data Collection

Organizations should adopt a comprehensive framework that addresses both immediate operational requirements and long-term sustainability. This framework should encompass technical, operational, and organizational elements, with particular attention to:

- **Resilience Planning**. Systems should be designed with multiple layers of redundancy and the ability to operate in degraded modes when necessary. This includes both technical systems and organizational processes, with clear protocols for maintaining essential operations under adverse conditions.

- **Resource Management**. Organizations must develop sophisticated approaches to resource allocation that can adapt to changing conditions while maintaining operational effectiveness. This includes not only physical resources but also human capital and technological capabilities.

- **Quality Assurance**. A robust quality assurance program should be integrated into all aspects of operations, with particular attention to validation of data collected under challenging conditions. This should include both automated systems and human oversight, with clear protocols for handling anomalous data.

Strategies for Risk Mitigation

Effective risk mitigation in hostile environments necessitates a comprehensive, multifaceted approach encompassing physical, digital, and operational risks. Organizations should implement the following measures:

- **Continuous Assessment**. Regular evaluation of both existing and emerging risks, coupled with mechanisms for swift response to evolving circumstances. This assessment should incorporate both technical and human intelligence sources, with well-defined protocols for escalating concerns and implementing countermeasures.

- **Adaptive Security**. Security measures should be adaptable and scalable, capable of responding to varying threat levels while ensuring operational efficiency. This encompasses physical security and cybersecurity measures, focusing on safeguarding sensitive data throughout its lifecycle.

Additional Future Directions and Possibilities

As the field continues to evolve, several key areas emerge as priorities for future research and development.

Despite significant progress, important gaps remain in our understanding of how best to collect and analyze data in hostile environments. These gaps include integration challenges.

More research is necessary on effective methods for integrating data from diverse sources while maintaining data quality and reliability. This includes both technical challenges of data fusion and operational challenges of managing multiple collection systems.

Validation methods need the development of more robust approaches for validating data collected under adverse conditions and they should be marked as a priority. This should include both automated validation systems and improved protocols for human verification of critical data.

Emerging Opportunities from Interdisciplinary Developments in Hostile Environment Operations

The intricate nature of hostile environment operations presents opportunities for cross-disciplinary research integrating insights from diverse fields. Promising areas of focus include:

- **Human-System Integration.** Research into more effective methods of integrating human judgment with automated systems, particularly in high-stress environments where both human and machine capabilities are subjected to extreme conditions.

- **Environmental Adaptation**. Studies of how both natural and artificial systems adapt to hostile conditions can provide valuable insights for enhancing the resilience of data collection systems.

The field of hostile environment data science stands at a pivotal moment, offering opportunities for substantial advancement through focused research and development. Priority areas for investigation include:

- **Adaptive Systems**. Development of more sophisticated systems capable of automatically adjusting to evolving conditions while ensuring data quality and operational security.

- **Sustainable Operations**. Research into methods for maintaining long-term operations in hostile environments, encompassing both technical sustainability and organizational resilience.

The future success of data collection in hostile environments hinges on our ability to address these challenges while leveraging emerging technologies and methodologies. Continued investment in research and development, coupled with meticulous attention to lessons learned from field operations, will be indispensable for advancing the field.

Appendix

Afghanistan

Afghanistan – 2002 – 2004 (War and First Elections)

The Soviet-Afghan War and its subsequent aftermath left Afghanistan in a state of profound instability and civil conflict. Following the Soviet withdrawal in 1989, various Mujahideen factions engaged in a protracted struggle for control of the country. The Taliban emerged as the dominant force by 1996, during which time Afghanistan experienced a significant increase in international isolation. This was primarily attributed to the Taliban's strict interpretation of Islamic law and its harboring of al-Qaeda, led by Osama bin Laden.

The September 11, 2001 terrorist attacks on the US, orchestrated by al-Qaeda from Afghanistan, led to an immediate international response. When the Taliban refused to extradite bin Laden, the US, with NATO allies, launched Operation Enduring Freedom on October 7, 2001.

Military Operation

The initial military campaign, combining US air power with Northern Alliance ground forces, proved effective in the early stages of the war. Major cities fell quickly: Mazar-i-Sharif on November 9, Kabul on November 13, and Kandahar on December 7. By December 2001, the Taliban regime collapsed, with many leaders fleeing to Pakistan's tribal areas.

Bonn Agreement

The swift military triumph paved the way for the Bonn Agreement, signed in December 2001. This pivotal document established a framework for political reconstruction in Afghanistan. The agreement established the Afghan Interim Authority, led by Hamid Karzai, who was elected as its chairman. The transitional period was meticulously crafted to pave the way for democratic governance, representing a significant departure from the oppressive rule of the Taliban.

The international community responded with unwavering resolve to Afghanistan's reconstruction. In January 2002, the Tokyo Conference witnessed donors pledging over $4.5 billion in aid for this endeavor. The United Nations authorized the International Security Assistance Force (ISAF) to provide security assistance within and around Kabul. Notably, NATO assumed command of ISAF in August 2003.

Despite initial optimism, the early reconstruction efforts encountered significant challenges. Although the Taliban had been defeated, they were not entirely eliminated. By 2003, they had commenced regrouping in Pakistan's tribal regions, launching increasingly sophisticated attacks against coalition forces and the newly established Afghan government. The challenging terrain along the Afghanistan-Pakistan border, coupled with intricate tribal allegiances and insufficient troop resources, rendered it arduous to prevent insurgent movements.

The reconstruction endeavor encountered numerous obstacles. Decades of conflict had wreaked havoc on much of Afghanistan's infrastructure and institutions. The country's economy was heavily reliant on opium production, which proved challenging to replace with viable alternatives. Corruption had become pervasive, undermining both reconstruction efforts and public confidence in the new government.

Despite these challenges, progress toward democracy continued. In December 2003, a Constitutional Loya Jirga (Grand Assembly) was convened, comprising representatives from diverse Afghan societies to engage in debates and ratify a new constitution. The resulting document, approved in January 2004, established Afghanistan as an Islamic republic with a robust presidential system while safeguarding fundamental rights, including women's rights and religious freedoms.

Elections

The inaugural presidential election in Afghan history was scheduled for October 9, 2004. Despite Taliban threats to disrupt the process, approximately 70% of registered voters participated. The election featured 18 candidates, including one female candidate, representing a notable departure from Afghanistan's historical political trajectory. While allegations of irregularities surfaced, international observers generally regarded the election as credible, acknowledging the arduous circumstances under which it was held.

Hamid Karzai

Hamid Karzai emerged victorious in the historic election, securing 55.4% of the vote and avoiding a runoff. This triumph marked Afghanistan's first democratically elected president, yet it also presented both achievements and challenges. While it represented a significant milestone in Afghanistan's democratic transition, it underscored the enduring influence of personalities over institutions in Afghan politics.

The election period unveiled both progress and persistent challenges. The participation of women as both voters and candidates represented a remarkable transformation from the Taliban era. However, security concerns deterred many Afghans, particularly in rural areas, from fully engaging in the political process. The election's success was somewhat mitigated by the continued strength of regional warlords and the diminished authority of the central government beyond Kabul.

The period from 2001 to 2004 represented a time of both significant accomplishment and sobering reality in Afghanistan. The fall of the Taliban, the establishment of novel political institutions, and the inaugural democratic election signified tangible progress. Nevertheless, these years also unveiled the formidable challenges confronting Afghanistan: persistent insecurity, inadequate governance, endemic corruption, and the indomitable resilience of the Taliban insurgency.

The Next Years

The international community's experience during this period would significantly shape its approach to state-building in Afghanistan for years to come. Initially, there was a focus on a light military footprint and a rapid political transition. However, this approach was recognized as insufficient for establishing a stable democracy in Afghanistan. The first presidential election, while historic, was not a culmination but rather the commencement of a protracted and intricate process of political development in Afghanistan.

Between 2020 and 2021, the withdrawal of US troops from Afghanistan was violent. And the country started to transition back until a full Taliban-controlled government was established.

The Iraq War

Background of the Iraq War (2002-2007)

Following the September 11, 2001 terrorist attacks, the Bush administration redirected its attention to Iraq as part of its broader "War on Terror." Although Iraq lacked a direct connection to the 9/11 attacks, the administration presented a multifaceted argument for military action against Saddam Hussein's regime. The central premise of their case was the assertion that Iraq possessed weapons of mass destruction (WMDs) and was actively developing more, including potential nuclear capabilities. The administration also emphasized alleged connections between Hussein's regime and al-Qaeda, although these links would later be contested. Furthermore, they highlighted Iraq's documented human rights violations and pattern of non-compliance with United Nations weapons inspectors as justifications for intervention.

Throughout 2002, the Bush administration intensified diplomatic efforts to garner international support for action against Iraq. A pivotal juncture occurred in September 2002, when President Bush addressed the United Nations General Assembly, compelling the organization to enforce its resolutions pertaining to Iraq's weapons programs. This diplomatic initiative culminated in November 2002, when the United Nations Security Council unanimously adopted Resolution 1441, granting Iraq a final opportunity to adhere to its disarmament obligations.

UN weapons inspectors, under the leadership of Hans Blix, resumed their presence in Iraq in November 2002 after a four-year hiatus. Their activities during this period yielded intricate and ultimately contentious outcomes. While the inspectors did not uncover any concrete evidence of active weapons of mass destruction programs, the United States and the United Kingdom governments asserted that Iraq was engaged in sophisticated deception to conceal its weapons and was not fully cooperating with inspection efforts.

The Invasion (March-May 2003)

The culmination of the path to war transpired on March 17, 2003, when President Bush issued an ultimatum to Saddam Hussein, compelling the Iraqi leader to vacate Iraq within 48 hours or face the imminent prospect of military intervention. Hussein's refusal to comply precipitated the commencement of Operation Iraqi Freedom on March 20, commencing with an intensive "shock and awe" campaign of aerial bombardment, subsequently followed by a coordinated ground invasion orchestrated by US and British forces.

The initial military campaign exhibited an overwhelming display of Coalition superiority. Coalition forces advanced with remarkable speed toward Baghdad, encountering Iraqi military resistance that proved largely ineffective in confronting the superior capabilities and tactics of the Coalition forces. The fall of Baghdad on April 9, a momentous occasion symbolized by the toppling of Saddam Hussein's statue in Firdos Square, marked a decisive juncture in the invasion. President Bush's "Mission Accomplished" speech aboard the USS Abraham Lincoln on May 1, 2003, was intended to signify the culmination of major combat operations, although this declaration proved premature.

Post-Invasion Period (2003-2004)

The immediate aftermath of the invasion exposed significant deficiencies in post-war planning. The Coalition Provisional Authority (CPA), established under Paul Bremer, made several critical decisions that had far-reaching consequences. The de-Baathification policy, which removed former party members from government positions, effectively dismantled a substantial portion of Iraq's civil service infrastructure. Similarly, the decision to disband the Iraqi army created a large pool of unemployed, armed men who later became the core of the insurgency.

These policies contributed to a rapidly deteriorating security situation. The power vacuum following the collapse of Hussein's regime led to widespread looting and destruction of critical infrastructure. Various insurgent groups emerged, drawing support from disenfranchised populations. Sectarian tensions between Sunni and Shia populations intensified, while anti-occupation sentiment grew among broad segments of Iraqi society.

During this period, the pursuit of weapons of mass destruction (WMDs) and Saddam Hussein occupied a significant portion of Coalition resources. The failure to locate WMDs dealt a substantial blow to Coalition credibility, although the capture of Saddam Hussein in December 2003 provided a notable triumph. However, the escalating insurgency and deteriorating security situation increasingly overshadowed these developments.

Insurgency and Civil Conflict (2004-2005)

The security situation deteriorated significantly during this period, marked by numerous major military confrontations and pivotal political developments that shaped the conflict. The First Battle of Fallujah in April 2004 and the Second Battle of Fallujah in November-December 2004 underscored the intensity of the insurgency and the challenges faced by Coalition forces. The Abu Ghraib prison scandal emerged during this time, severely compromising America's moral authority and exacerbating anti-Coalition sentiment. Concurrently, al-Qaeda in Iraq gained prominence among various militant groups operating within the country.

Political developments during this period included the transfer of sovereignty to the Iraqi Interim Government in June 2004, followed by the country's inaugural democratic elections in

January 2005. A constitutional referendum in October 2005 and parliamentary elections in December 2005 represented significant milestones in Iraq's political transition, although these processes also accentuated and, in some instances, exacerbated sectarian divisions.

Peak of Violence (2006-2007)

The bombing of the al-Askari mosque in Samarra in February 2006 marked a pivotal juncture in the Iraq conflict, precipitating unprecedented sectarian violence. This revered golden-domed shrine, sacred to Shi'a Muslims, was irreparably damaged by explosives detonated by Sunni extremists. While the immediate loss of life was minimal, the psychological and societal consequences were catastrophic, triggering a wave of sectarian violence that profoundly reshaped Iraq's social fabric.

Consequently, Baghdad descended into a state of near-constant civil war. Shi'a militias, notably the Mahdi Army under the leadership of Muqtada al-Sadr, retaliated against Sunni neighborhoods. Death squads affiliated with both sects engaged in systematic campaigns of intimidation, abduction, and murder. Previously harmonious neighborhoods experienced rapid demographic transformations as families relocated from areas where they constituted the religious minority. The violence was particularly acute in Baghdad, where centuries-old patterns of coexistence between Sunni and Shi'a residents were abruptly disrupted within a matter of months.

During this period, the sophistication of violent tactics escalated significantly. Improvised Explosive Devices (IEDs) became increasingly complex and lethal. Suicide bombings, frequently targeting crowded marketplaces and religious gatherings, occurred with alarming frequency. Torture became widespread, with bodies exhibiting signs of brutal treatment regularly appearing on Baghdad's streets. Mosque attacks multiplied, with both Sunni and Shi'a places of worship targeted in cycles of revenge.

The Iraqi security forces, themselves deeply infiltrated by sectarian elements, proved incapable or unwilling to stem the violence. Numerous police units were accused of participating in sectarian killings while wearing their uniforms. The situation was further exacerbated by militia members who had successfully integrated into the police and army, utilizing their positions to facilitate sectarian cleansing operations.

By late 2006, Baghdad had effectively been divided into isolated sectarian enclaves. Massive concrete barriers, affectionately known as "peace walls," were erected between Sunni and Shi'a neighborhoods. While these physical divisions contributed to a reduction in casual violence, they also institutionalized the sectarian segregation of the city. Residents required documentation to enter certain areas, and movement between neighborhoods became increasingly restricted and perilous.

The humanitarian crisis escalated, with monthly civilian death tolls surpassing 2,500, and some estimates suggesting over 3,000 deaths per month during the peak of violence. Hundreds of thousands of professionals fled, causing a brain drain and hindering Iraq's recovery. Essential services deteriorated as technicians and administrators left, and infrastructure repairs became difficult due to security concerns.

The US military, initially struggling to contain the violence, implemented strategic changes. The "Surge" strategy, announced in 2007, deployed an additional 20,000 troops, primarily in Baghdad and Anbar Province. Under General David Petraeus, the military adopted a new counterinsurgency doctrine emphasizing population protection over force projection. Troops moved from large bases to neighborhood outposts, maintaining a constant presence in violent areas.

Engagement with Sunni tribal leaders in Anbar Province was crucial to the new strategy. The "Awakening" movement, aided by American funding and support, saw former insurgents turn against al-Qaeda in Iraq. This alliance reduced violence in Sunni areas and cut off extremist support.

By late 2007, increased troop presence, new tactics, and tribal cooperation showed results. Violence levels decreased, though they remained high. Civilian casualties dropped by nearly 50% in some areas, and Baghdad began to normalize. Markets reopened, displaced families returned, and public spaces became accessible.

The sectarian violence in Iraq had profound and lasting effects. It disrupted centuries-old patterns of coexistence, leading to the breakdown of mixed marriages and a decline in intermarriage between sects. The psychological trauma inflicted on the population, especially children, had lasting consequences for Iraqi society. While segregation reduced immediate violence, it posed long-term challenges to national reconciliation and social cohesion.

Economic and Social Impact (2002-2007)

The war profoundly impacted Iraqi society, disrupting essential services like electricity and water supply. Damage to oil infrastructure hindered economic recovery, while cultural heritage sites' destruction was irreplaceable.

The human cost was staggering, with civilian deaths estimated between 50,000 and 600,000. Over 3,000 US military personnel lost their lives. Millions were displaced, creating a regional humanitarian crisis. Psychological trauma lingered across generations.

High unemployment and widespread corruption hindered economic recovery. Despite reconstruction aid, visible improvements were limited, and oil production struggled to recover.

International Ramifications

The war's impact extended far beyond Iraq's borders. Iran's influence in the region increased significantly, while regional stability deteriorated. Terrorist networks exploited the chaos to establish new footholds, and neighboring countries struggled to cope with refugee flows.

On a global scale, the war strained international relationships and sparked intense debates over international law and the concept of preemptive war. Questions about intelligence reliability and the shifting dynamics of global power would influence international relations for years to come.

Legacy and Lessons

The initial five years of the Iraq War imparted numerous lessons pertaining to contemporary warfare and nation-building. The paramount significance of comprehensive post-conflict planning became evident, as did the limitations of military power in achieving political objectives. The period underscored the detrimental impact of sectarian divisions on reconstruction endeavors and emphasized the paramount role of international cooperation in post-conflict scenarios.

The intelligence failures preceding the war catalyzed substantial changes outlined next in the gathering and analysis of intelligence. The period spanning from 2002 to 2007 profoundly shaped subsequent developments in Iraq and continues to exert influence on international relations and military doctrine in the present day. The war's impact on regional stability, counterterrorism initiatives, and international law remains of paramount importance in contemporary global affairs, serving as a pivotal case study in the intricate complexities of modern military intervention and post-conflict reconstruction.

The Iraq War catalyzed a paradigm shift in how intelligence organizations approach data collection and analysis. The conflict underscored several critical challenges in intelligence gathering and processing, prompting substantial advancements in data-driven methodologies.

Prior to and during the initial stages of the war, intelligence agencies encountered difficulties with information overload and data fragmentation. Different agencies independently collected vast quantities of data, but the tools and methods for processing and sharing this information were inadequate. This fragmentation of data and the absence of integration between agencies often resulted in missed connections and incomplete analysis.

The war catalyzed several significant advancements in data handling and analysis:

Intelligence agencies enhanced their text mining capabilities to process vast quantities of intercepted communications, reports, and documents in multiple languages. Natural Language Processing techniques were refined to effectively manage Arabic and other regional languages, thereby improving translation accuracy and the identification of crucial information in foreign language documents.

Pattern recognition algorithms were enhanced to more effectively identify anomalous behavior patterns in financial transactions, communications, and movement data. These systems demonstrated improved capabilities in distinguishing between routine activities and potential threats by analyzing intricate connections between seemingly disparate data points.

The imperative to process and analyze surveillance footage catalyzed substantial advancements in computer vision and video analytics. Machine learning models were designed to autonomously identify objects, individuals, and activities within video feeds, thereby augmenting the speed and efficiency of video intelligence analysis.

Data fusion techniques were augmented to amalgamate information from diverse sources, including human intelligence, signals intelligence, imagery, and open-source intelligence. This culminated in the development of more sophisticated systems capable of autonomously cross-referencing and validating data from disparate sources.

The experience underscored the paramount significance of predictive analytics in intelligence operations. Machine learning models were constructed to forecast potential hotspots of unrest or conflict based on a multitude of factors, such as social media activity, economic indicators, and population movements.

Nevertheless, these technological advancements also engendered novel challenges. The heightened reliance on automated systems prompted introspection regarding the equilibrium between human analysis and machine learning algorithms. Consequently, the intelligence community embarked on the development of novel protocols for validating machine-generated insights and ensuring human oversight of automated systems.

The war underscored the paramount significance of contextual analysis in data interpretation. While machines excelled in processing vast datasets, human analysts remained indispensable for comprehending cultural, historical, and societal nuances that machines could not fully grasp. This realization catalyzed the development of hybrid methodologies that seamlessly integrated machine learning capabilities with human expertise.

These lessons and advancements continue to shape the contemporary approach of intelligence agencies in data collection and analysis, emphasizing the necessity of integrated systems capable of handling substantial volumes of data while ensuring accuracy and contextual understanding.

The experience profoundly transformed how intelligence communities' approach big data, resulting in more sophisticated, integrated, and nuanced methodologies for data collection and analysis. Notably, it underscored the enduring value of human expertise in intelligence endeavors.

Index

www.ingramcontent.com/pod-product-compliance
Lightning Source LLC
Chambersburg PA
CBHW071254050326
40690CB00011B/2398